WITHOUT SURRENDER

ART OF THE HOLOCAUST

WITHOUT SURRENDER

ART OF THE HOLOCAUST

Nelly Toll

RUNNING PRESS
PHILADELPHIA, PENNSYLVANIA

Copyright © 1978 Running Press. All rights reserved under the Pan-American and International Copyright Conventions. Printed in the United States of America.

Canadian representatives: John Wiley & Sons Canada, Ltd.
22 Worcester Road, Rexdale, Ontario M9W 1L1

International representatives: Kaiman & Polon, Inc.
2175 Lemoine Avenue, Fort Lee, New Jersey 07024

9   8   7   6   5   4   3   2   1
Digit on right indicates the number of this printing.

Library of Congress Cataloging in Publication Data

Toll, Nelly.
    Without Surrender: Art of the Holocaust
    1. Holocaust, Jewish (1939-1945), in art.
2. Art, Jewish.   3. Holocaust, Jewish (1939-45).   I. Title.
N7417.6.T64   741.9'43   78-14859
ISBN 0-89471-055-9 library binding
ISBN 0-89471-054-0 paperback

Front and back cover illustrations: Buchenwald

''It All Depends On How You Look At It'' from *I Never Saw Another Butterfly,* edited by Hana Volavkova. Copyright © 1964. Used with the permission of McGraw-Hill Book Company.

Editor: Alida Becker
Interior design: Peter John Dorman
Cover design: James Wizard Wilson

Typography: Holland Seminar, with Serif Gothic Outline, by CompArt, Inc.,
    Philadelphia, Pennsylvania
Printed and bound by Printing Services, Inc., Philadelphia, Pennsylvania

This book may be ordered directly from the publisher.
Please include 50 cents postage.

TRY YOUR BOOKSTORE FIRST.

Running Press, 38 South Nineteenth Street, Philadelphia, Pennsylvania, 19103

To the Six Million; to the Family of Man; and to my own family, particularly my husband, whose emotional support enabled me to complete my work on this book.

Acknowledgments

I am greatly indebted to those survivors of the Holocaust who consented to share their deeply felt experiences with me.

My principal sources on the history of the Holocaust were Raul Hilberg's *The Destruction of the European Jews*, Nora Levin's *The Holocaust*, and Lucy Davidowitz's *The War Against the Jews*.

The poem ''It All Depends On How You Look At It'' is from a collection of children's work, *I Never Saw Another Butterfly*, edited by Hana Volavkova. Copyright © 1964. Reprinted with the permission of the McGraw-Hill Book Company.

Translations of the poem of the ninety-three maidens and the partisan song were graciously provided by Rabbi Ben Zion Bokser of the Forest Hills Jewish Center in New York.

Chana Magun of Haddon Township, New Jersey, was kind enough to translate the Yiddish ghetto song, ''My Name is Israelik.''

Foreword

As a rule, artists rarely provide satisfactory explanations for their deep interest in creative activity. Many can't even recall exactly when that interest began. Usually, it seems as though they've been occupied with a language of form as far back as they can remember.

Nelly Toll is different. She knows precisely where and when her attachment to art first took shape. It happened over thirty years ago in Europe during the Second World War, in 1941, when the tranquil security of her life in Poland was torn to shreds by the Nazi occupation.

She and her mother spent thirteen months in hiding. To pass the time, she read books smuggled in by the Polish family that looked after her, wrote in her diary, and made pictures on little sheets of paper with watercolors and a tiny brush. The idea of picturemaking was encouraged by Nelly's mother, who also functioned as an appreciative audience for the young artist. After all, even in seclusion a painter will respond to sympathetic attention.

One might expect Nelly Toll's paintings to reflect the grim realities and dreadful anxieties of her situation. But they don't. Filled with gentle tenderness and subtle detail, the pictures present settings that are largely remembered from her happy home life before the Nazis arrived. Most important, they project images of people—either involved in everyday, normal activities or serving as illustrations for such familiar childhood stories as *Uncle Tom's Cabin* and *Cinderella*—that assert a belief in the positive side of human nature. As such, they represent a triumph of the spirit over the most depressing and desperate circumstances. In her case, as with many others, oppression was transformed into a positive force, and the personal expression of art was put to work in a most beneficial way.

Now, as an adult, Nelly Toll continues to be creative in her painting and writing. Because of her own personal growth and development, it was inevitable for her to become deeply concerned with the art experiences of other people during the period of the Holocaust. The profound depth of that concern paved the way for this book. Few people are better qualified than Nelly Toll to carry out the task she set for herself. She has approached this critical inquiry with consummate sensitivity, sympathy, and passionate dedication.

Especially at this time in history, when many of the realities of the early 1940s are "conveniently" forgotten, it is more important than ever to have this body of artwork available. If people can learn from the past, they will surely be prepared to prevent the repetition of the Nazi horror. Indeed, this book is important because it is a significant reminder to people who would be free that they must be ever watchful in order to ensure that an episode like the Holocaust, and all the havoc it inflicted on the lives of innocent and defenseless people, shall never happen again.

Dr. Burton Wasserman
Professor of Art, Glassboro State College

A Note to the Reader

Anyone who is familiar with the history of the Holocaust will know that the art which has survived from that period is often not in the best condition. While every effort has been made to obtain the finest possible reproductions, the state of the originals has sometimes made this difficult. However, the work itself is too important to be omitted for this reason; indeed, its condition should be a reminder of the perils that were endured in order to preserve it.

This consideration leads to yet another. Whenever possible, I have provided documentation for the works in this book, but in many cases I have been unable to do so. The series of essays which constitutes my main text will give the reader some idea of the environment in which all this art, documented and undocumented, was produced.

—*N.T.*

Essays

A listing of source citations will be found on page 109.

Prisoner with a Crutch. Per Ulrich. Pencil
drawing. 21.0 x 15.0 cm. Camp Nuengamme.

"Art is that which is most real, the most austere of logic and the last judgment."

—Marcel Proust

"Works of art are indeed always products of having been in danger, of having gone to the very end in an experience, to where man can go no further."

—Rainer Maria Rilke

". . . art establishes the basic human truth, which must serve as the touchstone of our judgment."

—John F. Kennedy

ABOVE AND AT RIGHT: Drawn in Buchenwald.

Eight Million Alone

A NOTE ON THE HOLOCAUST

by Sidney H. Kessler
Professor of History
Glassboro State College

Who were the victims of the Holocaust? The general historian knows much more about their killers: the twelve-year terror state that was the Third Reich; the Nazi collaborators in every country from France to the Soviet Union, from Italy to the Baltic states; and the indifferent American and British democracies far away. They were eight million against the planet, isolated, stateless, unarmed for the most part, hated and hunted in every country, except by a handful of "righteous gentiles" whose names are inscribed forever in Jewish history.

Yes, we are accumulating more and more facts about the concentration camps, the subcamps, and the road camps—they are numbered in the hundreds now—and the enormous profit reaped by the Germans through this unprecedented exploitation of fellow human beings. We have the orders which created and destroyed the ghettos in Poland. Historical researchers are constantly seeking out Jewish hiding places, even in Berlin itself. There is

Drawn in Buchenwald.

now a strong indication that the secret bunkers of the Warsaw Ghetto held out even longer than anyone had suspected. But there is a comprehension lag concerning the people who were the objects of such a special obsession that their destruction often took precedence over winning the most devastating war in world history.

Jews were and are the People of the Book and of the land promised by God. Where the Nazis searched for "pure Aryans" even among the detested Poles and Gypsies—no Jew could be exempt from their "racial" exclusivism—Jews were and are a people who believe in egalitarianism. Foreigners are measured by the standards of the Torah, by their actions. Do they have courts of justice? Do they commit murder? Where the Nazis turned children against parents, and neighbor against neighbor, Jews clung to the holiness of each life, even life under unspeakable terms. There are Jews who argue that the greatest heroes were not those who engaged in armed resistance in ghettos, camps, and underground armies, but those who would not permit their parents to make their last journey alone.

These are the people whose fruit includes the artists of the Holocaust. Their creations are more than tributes to the dignity that was sustained even amid the degradation imposed by their oppressors. They are more than precious visual records of the victims of the Holocaust. They survive as windows into the ancient Jewish soul itself, the soul that lives on in the body of the state of Israel, the soul that remains "without surrender."

Drawn in Buchenwald.

Art of the Holocaust

Although the Holocaust represents one of the worst atrocities in the history of mankind, it is thought of by many only in terms of statistics, the brutal slaughter of six million lives, including a million children. Because this tragedy is so difficult to fathom, the art from the Nazi period stands at a remote distance from our everyday lives. Uncovered in various ghettos, concentration camps, and other hiding places, this very special art speaks of the drama, dignity, and courage of the victims. By defying the Nazis on paper, the artists of the Holocaust reflected the spiritual resistance of millions and transcended the horrors of their existence.

In a world of the most grotesque reality, these works of art have no need of embellishment. Arising for their own sake, they address us directly and bear witness to the fact that their creators defied the Nazi order and risked death by expressing their agony on paper. In spite of pain, degradation, and suffering, standing on the edge of life, the artists unfolded their experiences and gave evidence through their art of the enormity of the Nazi evil. Defying starvation and disease, they preserved their art and personal worthiness with astonishing fidelity and strength. The victims would not permit themselves to be chained in their aesthetic sight or allow their feelings of compassion for others to be polluted. Rising above their environment, they symbolically expressed their victory over death.

Felix Nussbaum was born on December 11, 1904 in Osnabrueck. He was trained as a professional artist and received the Academy of Fine Arts prize in 1931. In 1933, he emigrated to Belgium and married Felka Platek, a student colleague, in 1934 or 1935. Around 1940, he was deported to the detention camp at Gurs, France, in the Pyrenees. He managed to escape to Belgium in 1943, but was deported again in late 1943 or early 1944. He and his wife are believed to have been killed at Auschwitz.

Felix Nussbaum. 1940. Pastel of a scene at Camp Gurs.

ABOVE AND AT RIGHT: Drawn in Buchenwald.

20

Can one separate the story of this overwhelmingly in-human chapter of history from this art? Can one dissect the disaster that binds them together, find a thread that leads out of the labyrinth of hell and then divide that hell into independent areas of study? While we know that all art does not satisfy the same needs and interests, it is true nevertheless that the history of art is also the history of mankind.

Traditionally, the study of art history is based on scholarly inquiry into chronology, influences, descriptive characteristics, and stylistic evolution. A final critical analysis is based on the evidence of this accumulated research. The art of the Holocaust resists this type of study. Because of its unique roots and the circumstances under which it was executed, it does not fit the traditional demands of the discipline of aesthetics. But despite our lack of data and our inability to trace the evolutionary development of the artists, these fragmented works have earned an important place in the history of art.

The Holocaust artists made use of any found material, be it a stub of a pencil, a piece of coal, or any other tool. Their works have a power and simplicity whose roots can be traced all the way back to the earliest products of man's creative imagination. Ever since the cave paintings of Altamira and Lascaux and the funerary paintings of the Egyptians, artists have used symbols to serve the dead in the world of the hereafter, linking them with the living and permanently engraving their image throughout eternity.

Jewish intellectual and artistic expression dates back to the earliest times. Throughout the centuries, Judaism has held scholarship to be most sacred and morally valuable, and during various periods of Jewish history art has been

Drawn in Buchenwald.

an important means of enhancing a good and ethical life.

Throughout their modern ordeal, Jews have continued to find comfort in ancient Judaic symbols and talismans such as the Menorah and the Star of David. In the same way, the artists of the Holocaust attained symbolic immortality through their canvases of the ghettos and camps, using themes that perpetuated cultural links with the earliest days of their people's past.

In many ways, the art of the Holocaust represents an abstraction of a cruel reality, designed to create order out of chaos. Charged with power, it arouses deep emotions. In depicting an almost unimaginable odyssey of horror, this art maintains a remarkable artistic sensitivity, and even manages to convey a sense of beauty under the most deprived conditions.

These works are a response, both intellectual as well as intuitive, to the artists' eerie environments. Their utmost feelings are preserved on paper, and overcome religious, political, social, physical, and psychological barriers to remain symbols of integrity. The art of the Holocaust, which has survived despite the concentrated efforts of the Nazi regime, breaks down all the barriers that divide its creators from the rest of the world.

The camp artists created order out of a shambles; perceived shadows and lights; utilized line, composition, movement, and balance; and emerged to express the depths of their bruised and battered souls. These people of the ghettos and camps could not remain silent. Impelled by a sense of urgency, aware that each day might be their last, they silently recorded their own ''familiar'' world for those who were unaware of its existence. They extracted out of the ghettos and camps an historical truth which is preserved forever in their artwork.

Drawn in Buchenwald.

Rarely can an artist have a personal vision that expresses so powerfully the experiences of millions of his contemporaries. This Holocaust art, with its nightmarish gestures reminiscent of Bosch and Goya, and Picasso's ''Guernica,'' although created in secret and in widely scattered places, forms a powerful and cohesive body of work. It demonstrates the moral endurance, creative commitment, and spiritual resistance of individual artists, the few who rose like ashes in the wind and the many who were buried beneath the depths of the earth.

Their work serves as a permanent reminder of the horrors that took place and bears witness to the heroism of its creators. The artists of the Holocaust testified to the belief that man is capable of expressing his finest spirit even when pushed to the very limits of his existence. These brave artists transcended personal tragedy for much larger goals, and even today they address us directly with further proof that truth endures even in days that seem consumed with smoke.

It is my belief that if these artists of the dark days were able to see light through their creative forms, amid such a profoundly dehumanizing environment, then their art must be shared by all people today, and in the days to come. Although we cannot cross the barbed-wire fence that separates us from the cries and screams of their hell, the artists who perished in the gas chambers, the labor camps, and the ghettos have left us their souls on paper. This legacy expresses their last hope, the transfiguration of reality that symbolized their final embrace with life. History commands us not to forget—this art is the immortal symbol of that command.

Drawn in Buchenwald.

The Early Years

Prior to Adolf Hitler's rise to power, Germany's poets, musicians, architects, and artists represented a vital aesthetic force. In the nineteen twenties the innovative Bauhaus movement, which embraced not only architecture but the whole range of the visual arts, was recognized throughout Europe and rapidly became a major international influence. The school at Dessau, with its celebrated faculty, attracted such well-known artists as Kandinsky, Klee, and Marc.

German artists were also active in the Dada movement which was founded in Zurich, Switzerland, in 1916. "Dada," a French kindergarten word meaning "hobbyhorse," expressed a state of mind rather than a style, and its proponents rebelled against prevailing social values. Its members included George Grosz in Berlin, Kurt Schwitters in Hanover, and Max Ernst in Cologne.

Although the artists of the Dada movement were at times the most outspoken, throughout the twenties artists all across Europe reacted to the growing political turmoil in Germany. Even before the Nazis came to power, many had produced artwork that symbolically expressed their fear of what was to come.

Otto Dix of the Neue Sachlichkeit, *the School of the New Objectivity, was greatly influenced by nineteenth-century romanticism, the German Gothic tradition, and the trench warfare of World War I. His work ranged in style from expressionism to dadaism. His new fantasy*

After the German invasion and the inevitable collapse of France, the machinery of Nazi destruction swept south. In the early stages of the occupation, the collaborationist Vichy government was reluctant to turn in French citizens who happened to be Jews. But the French were subjected to increasing amounts of propaganda and, despite a certain uneasiness about the persecutions, they began to show a willingness to collaborate which surprised even the Germans, confirming their belief that no one in Europe really "wanted" the Jews. Under Theodor Dannecker, Adolf Eichmann's lieutenant from the *Sicherheitsdienst,* or *S.D.,* various administrative offices specializing in the deportation and extermination processes were established.

With efficient speed, Jewish businesses were confiscated and Jews were ordered to wear armbands marked with the yellow Star of David. A card index system was compiled listing the name, address, nationality, and occupation of every known Jew in Paris. Medical examinations designed to detect "Jewish" facial and physical characteristics were conducted at numerous hospitals and clinics.

(Caption continues on page 30.)

Gurs 1941. Liesel Felsenthal. Illustrated diary, watercolor in a nonbound book format. 2½ x 3 inches.

From 7 to 8, it's time to get coffee.

From 8 to 9, in the bathroom.

GURS
1941

LIESEL FELSENTHAL

VON 7-8ʰ heisst is KAFFEE holen

VON 8ʰ-9ʰ im Waschraum bei der Körper-pflege.

also included minutely detailed, realistic canvases peopled with machinelike monsters which appeared to symbolize the surreal perpetrators of the oncoming evil.

Max Beckmann, a leading exponent of expressionism, was not politically oriented, but he too responded through his art, which was labeled "magic reality" by the critics of the twenties. Influenced by fifteenth-century woodcuts and Dutch painting, Beckmann's "Descent from the Cross," with its distorted and emaciated figures, provided a grim premonition of the concentration camps' "living corpses."

Emil Nolde, a German expressionist who left the Brüke movement, reflected the impending crisis with passionate intensity. His rapid, massive slashes of violent color became part of a chilling fantasy landscape. During his solitary studies in Munich, Paris, and Dachau (which later became infamous for its concentration camp), Nolde continued to paint with deeply felt religious dedication.

In the late twenties and the early thirties, the Nazi presence was felt by Jewish painters throughout Europe. One of the most prominent was Marc Chagall, who was influenced by Pascin, Soutine, the Fauves, and the cubists, and frequently juxtaposed his Parisian existence with childhood memories of his poor Jewish-Russian background. Later, he turned to spiritual and religious themes. Before escaping from occupied France to the United States in 1941, he produced an impressive series of illustrations for Gogol's Dead Souls.

Like many other artists, Jacques Lipschitz, a student of the Ecole des Beaux Arts in Paris, came under the influence of Picasso's cubism. His massive sculpture

The Jewish population panicked. False passports and Aryan papers were in great demand. When they could not be obtained, families frantically sought ways to hide. Some were sheltered by Christian friends, others escaped to the mountains or the countryside.

One of the first major actions in France was the deportation of naturalized Polish Jews in 1941. After internment at Drancy, a main French transit camp, they were shipped on to Auschwitz. In 1942, over 4,000 children were penned up in the Velodrome d'Hiver, a converted sports stadium in Paris, until trains became available for their journey to the camps. Out of thousands of Parisian Jews who were rounded up and sent to Auschwitz, only a handful survived.

These deportations were given the highest priority, despite the competing needs of the military; the transport of Jews from France to the death camps often interfered with that of soldiers and military supplies to the front. Even on the eve of Hitler's defeat, when every train was critical to the army's survival, the Germans

(Caption continues on page 32.)

From 9 to 10, the beds are aired.

From 10 to 11, at the canteen.

From 11 to 12, we wash the laundry.

From 12 to 1 (12 to 13), at the stove.

von 9–10ⁿ Kommen die Betten herous

von 10ⁿ–11ⁿ um der cantine

von 11ⁿ–12ⁿ Waschen wir die Wäsche

von 12ⁿ–13ⁿ um öfnen

"Prometheus Struggling with the Vulture" became a symbol of the victory of light over darkness, and his "Bull and Condor," produced in 1932, became a prophetic depiction of German brutality. Realizing the Nazis' intent to destroy the Jews of Europe, Lipschitz and his wife hid in the hills of southern France until they too were able to escape to the United States.

George Grosz (who changed his name from Gross to Grosz, a less German-sounding name) castigated the sinister forces of the military and became actively involved in anti-Nazi propaganda. His earliest antiwar caricatures are best exemplified by "Germany, a Winter's Tale" (1917-1919), which paints a kaleidoscopic portrait of Berlin, complete with the menacing expression of generals, officers, and greedy burghers. This powerful composition of broken objects and superimposed figures was probably inspired by a Heinrich Heine poem which attacked the Prussian military.

George Grosz's work depicted the Nazis as instruments of hate and evil. During the thirties he produced savage caricatures of Hitler, and amassed a powerful portfolio of antiwar drawings. Grosz also used theater to express his opposition to the Nazis, creating stage designs for the controversial antiwar play "The Adventures of Good Soldier Schweik." All this activity—but particularly the fact that Grosz was a Jew—finally made it necessary for him to flee to the United States with his wife.

Oscar Kokoschka, an artist from Vienna who was known for his hallucinatory and often morbid portraits,

denied a French request that a group of Jewish children be diverted to orphanages. Instead, Eichmann managed to provide railroad cars so that the youngsters could be shipped to Drancy and then to Auschwitz.

Among the most infamous detention camps was Gurs, in the Pyrenees, one of the largest camps in France, which served as a way station on the route "to the east." Liesel Felsenthal, a young girl from the Palatinate, was among those interned there. When many other inmates fell dead from weakness, hard labor, and starvation in the cold winter days of 1941, she used her diary to preserve her sanity.

Instead of evoking the horrors she had seen, the pictures in her diary portray simple daily activities. But hers was not merely a tale of dormitory experiences, it was a means of survival.

There is no record of what happened to Liesel Felsenthal. It is believed that she perished in one of the Nazi extermination centers, possibly Auschwitz. Only the pages of her diary can tell us her story.

From 1 to 2 (13 to 14), fetching the bread.

From 2 to 3 (14 to 15), at the ticket counter.

From 3 to 4 (15 to 16), we pick up the food.

From 4 to 5 (16 to 17), hanging up the wash.

von 13ʰ–14ʰ Brot -
holen

von 14ʰ–15ʰ am
Ticketschalter

von 15ʰ–16ʰ Zurücker-
holen

von 16ʰ–17ʰ wird die Wäsche
aufgehängt

gave vent to his deeply felt emotions in a highly expressionistic style. In 1934, Kokoschka fled from Vienna to Prague and then to London. The same year, his public work was confiscated by the Nazis as "degenerate."

Max Ernst, a leading surrealist painter who had moved to France in 1922, was also publicly humiliated and forbidden to show his work in Germany until he was cured of his "degeneracy." Like many of his compatriots, Ernst later emigrated to the United States.

*　　　*　　　*

It is ironic that Adolf Hitler himself had originally aspired to a career as an artist. Although his drawings had been rejected by the Vienna Academy of Fine Art in October 1907, he continued to apply. His persistence was not rewarded; in fact, one of his early teachers described him as a poor student, whose work lacked self-discipline. Despite these discouraging assessments of his talent, Hitler borrowed money from his mother and attempted to support himself by copying picture postcard views of Vienna. Needless to say, his work never gained recognition.

Instead, Hitler exerted his influence on the arts through the political arena. As his forces gained control, the cosmopolitan climate in Germany was engulfed by nationalistic Nazi propaganda. His government abhorred expressionism, impressionism, cubism, surrealism, futurism, and other abstract forms of art. Anything not rooted in what the Nazis saw as classicism was considered to be degenerate. In particular, the depiction of poverty, cruelty, and the pathos of the human condition was strictly

From 5 to 6 (17 to 18), fetching water.

From 6 to 7 (18 to 19), dinner is ready. Hurrah!

From 6 to 7 (18 to 19), a little chat.

From 8 to 9 (20 to 21), we're busy playing card games with the men.

von **17** – **18** Wasser- holen

von **18** – **19** Das Essen kommt – Hurra!

von **18** – **19** Ein kleines Schwätzchen

von **20** – **21** Sind wir mit inneren Spielen beschäftigt

outlawed. Artists who would not adhere to these "aesthetic reforms" were subject to humiliating ridicule, persecution, and eventual deportation to concentration camps.

The government proceeded rapidly in its "purification" of the arts, confiscating what was branded as "Jewish vermin" art and "decadent" non-Jewish modern art. Under the direction of Hitler's propagandist, Joseph Goebbels, posters were hung all over Berlin denouncing the Jews and espousing the ideal of the Aryan race. The Nazis' emotional appeal to the public used attractive placards that urged the people's support of the Hitler Youth and its female counterpart, the Bund Deutscher Mädchen. Some of the posters featured the Führer himself heroically slaying Jews or Bolsheviks; others portrayed helmeted storm troopers marching through the streets with clenched fists. In addition, pro-Nazi murals and paintings became part of the decor of many public buildings.

Following Hitler's dictum that brutality and physical force were to be glorified, Hans Schweitzer-Mjölnir, a prominent Nazi artist, created powerful, exaggerated depictions of the storm troopers' fighting spirit and Herculean strength. Other pro-Nazi artists portrayed scenes of the Führer's glory by illustrating Hitler's slogans and quotations.

In contrast to the works encouraged by the government, modern art—the "art of moral decay" and "decadent expressionism"—posed a threat which was answered with an increasingly elaborate propaganda campaign. Important works of modern art were confiscated by

From 9 to 10 (21 to 22), talk of love.

From 10 to 11 (22 to 23), the castle is calling.

From 11 to 12 (23 to 24), we're going to bed.

From 12 to 7 (24 to 7), quiet all around. Only the rats play their game.

VON 21ʰ-22ʰ Liebesgeflüster

VON 22ʰ-23ʰ Die Hoch-
Burg ruft

VON 23ʰ-24ʰ wir legen
uns zu
Bett.

VON 24ʰ-7ʰ Ruhe überall
nur die Ratten
treiben ihr Spiel.

ABOVE AND AT RIGHT: Drawn in Buchenwald.

the state, and the Nazis used these paintings and sculptures to stage exhibits which purportedly exposed "anti-Nazi" attitudes.

Through these shows, Nazi propagandists made a decisive attempt to blame Germany's ills on what they saw as the artistic decadence of Jews and their negative influence on society at large. In 1933, a Nazi exposition in Stuttgart called "November Spirit Art in the Service of Disintegration" was directed against Beckmann, Chagall, Dix, and Grosz. Another exhibition, in Mannheim, focused on "cultural Bolshevism" and featured Grosz's "Ecce Homo" series, which was labelled with propagandistic slogans.

A major "degenerate art" show in Munich was opened by Hitler himself in 1937. The exhibit catalogue did not engage in subtleties; George Grosz's drawings were accompanied by a text alluding to the sexual corruption and moral degeneration of his work.

The Munich show marked the onset of Joseph Goebbels' concentrated effort to eradicate modern art in Germany. Dr. Goebbels declared that those artists who did not wish to glorify the Nazis would be appropriately dealt with, and from that time nationalistic propaganda was increasingly linked with attacks on expressionism and claims of a Jewish-Bolshevik conspiracy. The government's attack moved into high gear.

Goebbels' campaign resulted in the murder of over twenty painters and the confiscation of approximately sixteen thousand works of art. Some were sold abroad to help finance Hitler's museum in Linz; others were burned or appropriated by the Minister of Aviation, Hermann Goering. On Hitler's personal orders, art critic

Gela Seksztejn was born in 1907 and died in Treblinka in 1942. Like other artists who were imprisoned in the Warsaw Ghetto, she contributed paintings to the archives of the *Oneg Shabbat*, or Sabbath Celebrants. This secret group, organized by Dr. Emmanuel Ringelblum, collected materials which documented the destruction of Poland's Jews. Hidden underground, many of these records were recovered after the liberation.

When Gela Seksztejn was called for "resettlement" in 1942, she had no illusions about her fate. Before her departure from the ghetto, she wrote these final words: "Today I stand on the border between life and death. I know that I must die, so I bid farewell to my comrades and to my paintings. Be well, my friends. You who survive, the Jewish nation, must teach the world about what happened here. Such a tragedy must never take place again."

Gela Seksztejn. Warsaw Ghetto.

 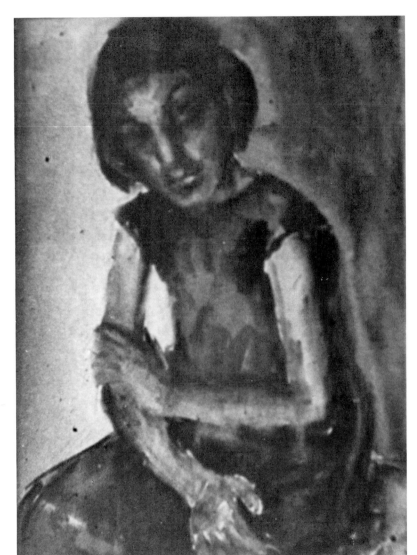

Einstazstab Rosenberg conducted a search for valuable Jewish-owned furniture and art objects in occupied France. Once shipped from Paris to Germany, these treasures were catalogued by Rosenberg and became part of the private collections of Hitler and Goering.

At the same time, other collections were being amassed in secret by Europe's captive Jews—drawings and paintings that bore witness to the Nazis' terrible crimes. At the risk of savage punishment, artists in the ghettos and camps created and preserved these testaments to the Holocaust.

Why, from its very beginnings, did the Nazi regime provoke such violent attacks on the arts? And what was the meaning of artistic expression in such a society? Dr. Robert Blumberg, a Philadelphia psychiatrist who has treated many survivors of the concentration camps, has this explanation:

''Germany needed to see Hitler as a righteous, avenging angel—and Hitler had an equally deep need to fill such a role. In fulfilling these needs, the most sinister forces of propaganda were unleashed and took dead aim at all the noblest urges of the human spirit. It is, then, not surprising that artistic expression was a prime target.

''The sicker the state, the more pervasive and extreme are its repressive measures against genuine expression. The German state was so very sick, and its Nazi leadership so efficient at maintaining that sickness, that finally the only significant number of people capable of artistic expression were in concentration camps. In other words, if any works that could be truly considered art came from the German society of that time, they almost certainly had to come from a group of condemned Jews.''

Drawn in Buchenwald.

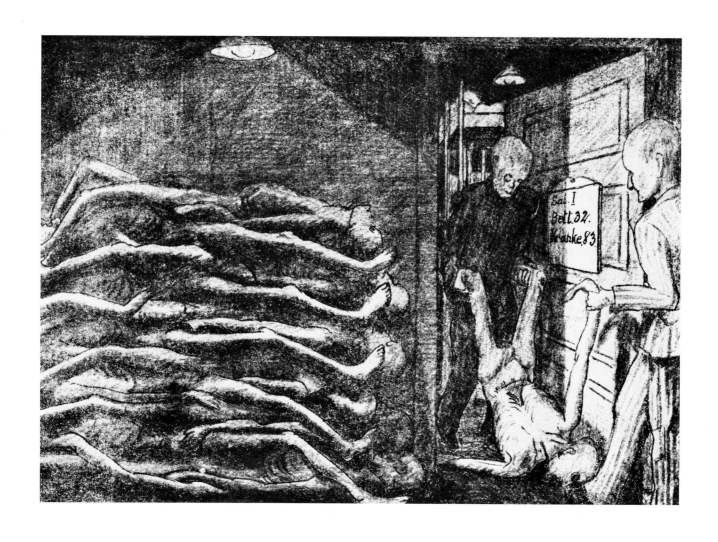

Harvest of Death. Hans P. Sorensen. Pencil
drawing. 19.0 x 28.0 cm. Camp Nuengamme.

Punishment Drill. Hans P. Sorensen. India ink
drawing. 30.0 x 45.0 cm. Camp Nuengamme.

The Camps

Concentration camps were a part of the Nazi reality from the first years of Hitler's rise to power. As early as 1933, there were fifty in existence—among them the infamous Dachau, Sachsenhausen, Mauthausen, and Buchenwald. Supervision of the camps' terrorized slave laborers was entrusted to carefully selected Death's Head units of the S.S., whose members were known for their ruthlessness and brutality.

The Nazi program for establishing their "racially pure" state also included euthanasia centers for deformed children, the incurably sick, and the mentally ill. These centers were camouflaged as foundations and nursing homes in order to deceive the families of patients, who were periodically informed of the "progress" of their loved ones—or notified, usually with an expression of "sincere sorrow," of a sudden death. Children were usually killed by lethal injections, adults by gas asphyxiation. A new code was devised for this operation and its symbols, "14f. 13," were attached to falsified lunacy certificates in the files of Jewish prisoners.

The horrors of the euthanasia centers, slave labor camps, and Nazi medical research installations increased over the years. A highly efficient euthanasia program had gone into effect in the fall of 1939, and by the end of 1941 mass murder by gas on the "incurably sick" and "insane" was widespread. In the face of public opposition from non-Jewish families, Hitler discontinued the program for gentiles. However, euthanasia on healthy Jews continued unabated.

Hitler's conquest of Europe engulfed the Jewish population and sealed most of their escape routes. Despite the occupation, Denmark welcomed many refugees, and her citizens used whatever means they could to oppose the Nazis.

Resistance groups were formed to combat the Nazi programs, and the Evangelical Lutheran Church reflected its true Christianity by distributing blank baptismal certificates. Because of the nation's vehement opposition to the surrender of the Jewish population, and because Danish food supplies and industry were vital to the German war effort, the Nazis proceeded with caution.

When door-to-door searches were finally scheduled, the Danes ignored threats of reprisals and mobilized all their resources, setting in motion a highly organized rescue operation. Private cars, trucks, vans, and taxis were made available as Jews were secretly transported to hospitals, churches, stores, factories, schools, and private homes. Fishermen provided boats to smuggle Jewish citizens to Sweden after a hasty agreement was negotiated by the Danish government.

Although the majority of the Jews in Denmark escaped death, many were caught and sent to the camps. The work of some of these "camp brothers" from Nuengamme has been preserved in the Danish National Museum. There it serves as permanent testimony to the heroism of those who resisted the Nazi terror and the humanitarianism of the Danish people.

Dying People (from the crematory). Per Ulrich. March 29, 1945. Pencil drawing. 14.5 x 10.5 cm. Camp Nuengamme.

fra krumatoriet

Arbeitslied. Buchenwald.

Drawn in Buchenwald.

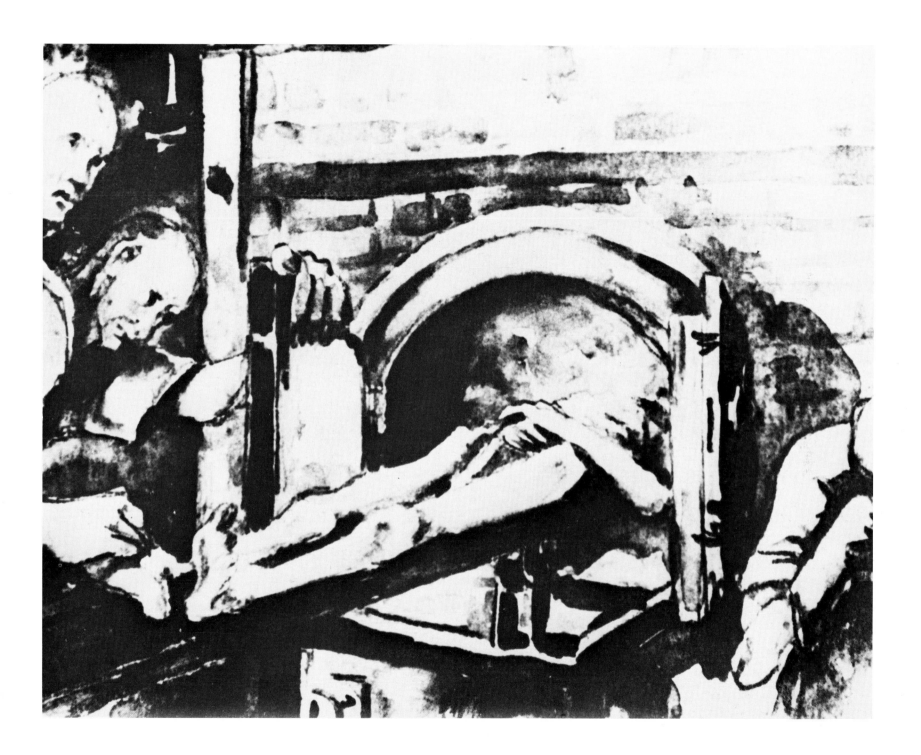

The introduction of gassing apparatus to various concentration camps created death centers that aided the Nazis in even more rapid and efficient ways of extermination. In the spring of 1942, gas chambers appeared in Belzec, Chelmno, Sobibor, Lublin, Treblinka, and Auschwitz. The slave laborers of other camps who somehow survived hunger, brutal beatings, raging disease, and sheer physical exhaustion were eventually deported to these and other installations.

Jewish men, women, and children were rounded up from all over Europe. As laborers for the Nazis, they were exploited in the most brutal manner—and while non-Jewish prisoners continued to work (and die) in the same labor camps, only Jews were sent to the gas chambers. Even if a Jewish prisoner could survive the inhuman conditions and prolong his life a day or a week longer, he was never sure when the next influx of prisoners would begin to "crowd" the camp, forcing another "evaluation" of candidates for the gas chambers. The murder of Jews had become a Nazi obsession.

Had the camps been bombed, more of their inmates might have survived. Although the Allies destroyed factories, industrial plants, and other installations crucial to the German war effort, places like Auschwitz were not on their list of targets. And so a chilling shade of indifference was cast over the fate of the victims. The Allies watched in silence as the mass murders took place.

When the Russians liberated the camps, the world was shocked at their discovery. The only remains of humanity in the crematoria—with their furnaces, drums of Zyklon B gas, and steel retorts of carbon monoxide—were human bones and ashes.

Drawn in Buchenwald.

Auschwitz, one of the largest extermination centers, provides a grim example of what life was like in the camps. Located near the city of Krakow in Poland, it had thirty-nine branches and work camps and was divided into three sections, Stammlarger, Birkenau, and Auschwitz. At the Nuremberg trials, Rudolph Hess reported that about two and a half million men, women, and children were exterminated at Auschwitz; another half million died of disease, hunger, and torture.

There were few means of escape from the camp. All the boundaries of its many branches were surrounded with a twelve-foot-high electrified wire fence which was watched continuously from towers manned by S.S. guards.

Those who were not gassed immediately upon arrival had a number burned on their left arm as a means of identification. A human being became a number without a name, a life, or a future once he arrived in Auschwitz, the valley of death. Each inmate had to give up all his personal clothing—like the flesh and bones of the victims, this was processed for use by the Nazis—and was given a camp uniform with an identification number matching the tattooed number on his arm.

The working day on this edge of existence consisted of sixteen hours of hard labor. Poor food was accompanied by rampant disease. Torture and sexual sadism were common.

Jewish prisoners were often forced to demean themselves. Accompanied by cudgels and sticks wielded by the S.S., Jewish musicians were made to play continuously while other inmates danced, turning and turning in time to the music until they collapsed in total exhaustion. At other times, spurred on by whips, prisoners were

Bertolan Gondor drew these cartoons during March, April, and May of 1944, when the Hungarian labor camps were taken over by the Germans and their prisoners began to be deported to Auschwitz.

Although Gondor's work is less crude, his style is reminiscent of that of Czech cartoonist Joseph Lada, who illustrated Jaroslav Hasek's ''The Adventures of Good Soldier Schweik.'' Both depict the extremities of life and man's brutality to his fellow man, but, unlike Lada, Gondor was forced to camouflage his intent. The postcards he sent to his wife had to pass through Nazi censors.

Gondor's drawings reflect his strength, spirit, and will to survive. Filled with quiet despair, he still manages to avoid self-pity. His art stitches together the remnants of a life that cannot reveal its true face and uses clever images to suggest the realities of the camp.

PAGES 53 THROUGH 59. Bertolan Gondor. Postcards. March 11, 1944 through May 24, 1944.

PAGE 53. TRANSLATION:

My dear little heart,
Although my feet are surely getting shorter from wear, my love for you can only grow. My dear, take care of yourself, don't worry about me. I'm well, and, as you can see, my sense of humor hasn't disappeared. I'm thinking only of you continuously, my beloved. I miss the Bans, too.
—Bard

PAGE 58. TRANSLATION:

My love, a greeting, a kiss, a snapshot from your Bui.

1944 március 11.
III. 11. 44

Drága Kicsi Szívem,
nagy túrázásod között gondolok Rád
Volna a Lábaim bírónyára rövidebbre

hontad de a kedvetem irántad csak
fokozódott. Drágám vigyázz Magadra
miattam ne aggódj mert én jól va-
gyok és mint látod nem hiányzik
a jó kedélyem. Csak Rátok gondolok
Édes. Banékat is csókolom
Bárd

56

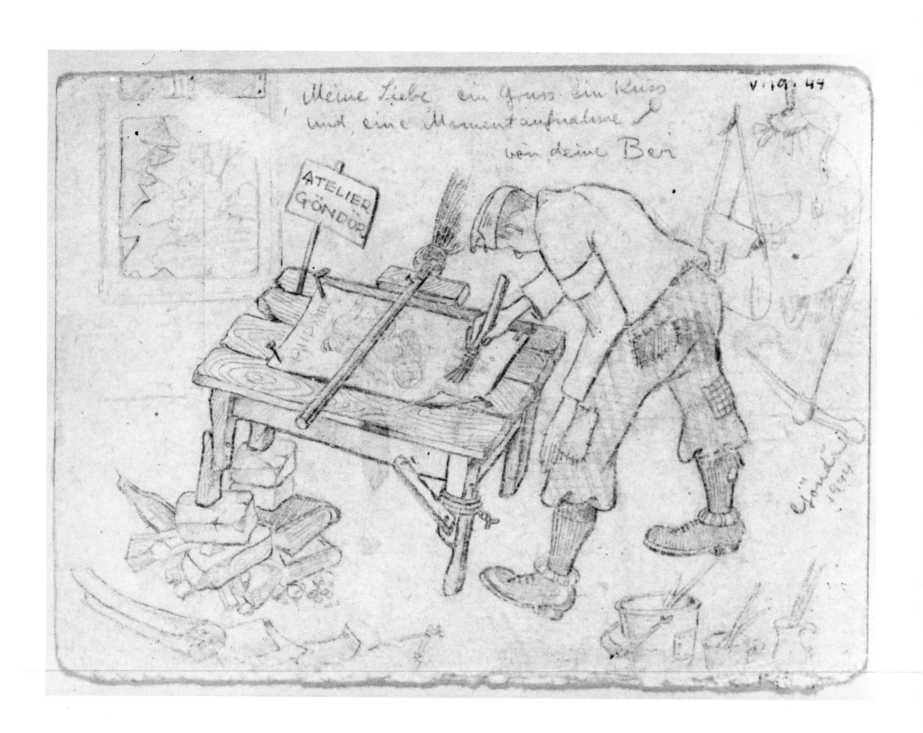

58

made to hop on bent knees like frogs, only to be lashed harder as the strains of the music quickened.

Holding onto their humanity despite the terrorization, professional musicians defiantly produced secret compositions for the very instruments on which they performed for the Germans. Their "official" concerts lasted until they fell dead from hard labor or were gassed.

All of the conditions in the camps were, of course, designed to kill. For the inmates, the coming of each new day represented a victory of life over death. To live meant to be able to work. Those inmates who were employed by the I.G. Farben factory or the Krupp armament works made a constant effort to appear healthy. If they failed to pass the regular inspections, their chances of remaining alive were nil. A camp doctor had only to point a finger to the left and the "unhealthy" victim was facing the last hour of his life. Anyone who was not able to work was destined for the gas chambers. Over five hundred lives could be diverted in only fifteen minutes.

As the extermination program progressed and new trainloads of prisoners continued to arrive daily, the killing accelerated to keep pace. A specially selected group of "strong men," usually chosen by the Nazis from the new arrivals, was responsible for the most cruel work: removing the corpses from the gas chambers and burning or burying them. Even for the men of this special unit, who had no choice but to obey their captors, life did not last long. When their strength gave out, they too were subject to the selection process.

*   *   *

Unlike camps like Dachau and Auschwitz, the town of Terezin in Czechoslovakia was a Nazi "showplace." But

Henri Pieck. Buchenwald.

60

it gave only a cheap illusion of freedom. Anyone who cared to look carefully would not have been fooled.

Visitors were steered through hastily cleaned-up grounds and freshly painted exteriors which seemed, as Red Cross Commission members reported, to have been decorated ''with consideration for the happiness and peace of mind'' of the inmates. Terezin's population, which consisted of families with children, old people, and Mischlinge (men and women of mixed marriages), were in constant fear of reprisals and kept silent even as the Red Cross was escorted through their midst.

Their helplessness is perhaps best expressed by this poem composed by Miroslav Košek, a young boy who spent almost two years in Terezin and died at Auschwitz on October 19, 1944.

Terezin is full of beauty.
It's in your eyes now clear
And through the street the tramp
Of many marching feet I hear.

In the ghetto at Terezin,
It looks that way to me,
Is a square kilometer of earth
Cut off from the world that's free.

Death, after all, claims everyone,
You find it everywhere.
It catches up with even those
Who wear their noses in the air.

The whole, wide world is ruled
With a certain justice, so
That helps perhaps to sweeten
The poor man's pain and woe.

Boris Taslitsky. Drawing on paper used for target practice. Buchenwald.

Few of the inmates knew that Terezin was merely a temporary stop on the way to the gas chambers. The Nazis' mass deportation programs, camouflaged as "labor transports," constantly shifted prisoners from place to place. Groups of prisoners were shipped in and out, their movements always shrouded in secrecy.

Many pieces of art from Terezin perished along with their creators; others outlived the Holocaust. When a transport left for Auschwitz with its doomed cargo, drawings that had been left behind were often hidden. After the liberation, survivors turned over the cache of poems, diaries, and art to the Jewish Museum in Prague. Some of this work was edited by Hana Volavkova and published by the museum in 1962 in a volume entitled Children's Drawings and Poems, Terezin 1942-44. *The American edition was called* I Never Saw Another Butterfly.

The landscape of the camps, those monstrous islands of death, transformed the surreal into the most gruesome reality. The artist inmates showed their fellow prisoners, with their gaunt faces and sluggishly drooped heads, moving their feet without stopping, their exhausted bodies filled with pain. Amid the cruel laughter of their tormentors, they staggered in their last funeral march. But despite their delerium, they still remained human. Unlike their captors, they did not become animals; the stronger helped the weaker. Humanity prevailed.

It seems a miracle that there should be such a stirring for culture at a time of such pitiless death. Perhaps only through art were those in the camps able to overcome, even momentarily, their existence. Every scrap of paper, every piece of coal or pencil stub, was a treasure which, like the works of art, had to be hidden. The fragments of

Drawn in Buchenwald.

these compositions that remain can all too often only be labelled "artist unknown."

Despite its anonymity, this work speaks to us with the memory of the artists' desperation. Today, the landscape of the camps, their tortured living skeletons turned to ashes, has silently sunk into the depths of Hades. Green grass covers the sins of the past, wild flowers spring back to life where once there was only barbed wire. The birds, strangers to such human suffering, fly through the blue skies, and children watch the rhythmic passage of a butterfly. Such peaceful scenes cover the black earth of the past's nightmarish reality.

The voices of these paintings and drawings, the only legacy of their vanished creators, cry out and demand to be seen. They lead us into an aesthetic arena that has never been portrayed before in the history of mankind, surpassing all the tragic events ever depicted in our art.

The artist of the camps was determined to let us glimpse his last brutal descent to death. Through the mirror of his creativity we can perhaps in a fleeting moment become one with the specter.

The Polish Ghettos

In October 1939, Adolph Hitler gave Heinrich Himmler, who was already head of the dreaded secret police, the S.S., total authority in occupied Poland. Himmler's chief objectives were the elimination of the Polish elite, the incorporation of the civilian population into Germany's work force, and the absolute and systematic extermination of the country's Jews. In Poland, as was true

Drawn in Buchenwald.

ABOVE AND AT RIGHT: Drawn in Buchenwald.

throughout the rest of Europe, this last goal could not be accomplished without the cooperation of the populace. For the most part, Poland offered Hitler her support.

As Reich Commissioner for Strengthening German Folkdom, Himmler could determine whether or not certain Poles were fit for "assimilation" into the Reich. However, Poland's Jews were turned over to Reinhard Heydrich, whose Einsatzgruppen, a special mobile killing squad, became noted for its atrocities. New racial laws were speedily instituted, and a propaganda campaign was begun.

Shortly after Hitler's invasion, Jews were herded into small sections of various cities that were isolated from the non-Jewish community—the ghettos. Already overcrowded, conditions in these areas became even worse as Jews were shipped in from all over the country. The ghetto populations quickly began to suffer from hunger, disease, and exposure to the freezing temperatures. Epidemics, fed by poor sanitation, devoured the bodies of young and old alike. Terror and death reigned supreme.

Community leaders in the ghetto courageously refused the Germans' demands for lists naming children under ten and adults over sixty-five. Realizing that deportations to the labor camps were imminent, some terror-stricken mothers and fathers tried to hide their children in attics or cellars. Others attempted to smuggle the children out of the ghetto and hide them with gentile families. Few of these ploys succeeded. The Nazi stranglehold on the ghettos tightened.

Determined to resist, refusing to give up the bits and pieces of their broken lives, the Jews cared for their sick and supported schools for their children, including classes in music, poetry, and painting. Ignoring their physical

The destruction of Hungarian Jewry under the leadership of Eichmann and the *Sondereinsatz Kommando* was marked by sadism and ruthlessness. Despite protests from the clergy and the intellectual community, many Hungarians aided the process of annihilation. Neither the Nazis' anti-Jewish laws nor the massacres that followed met a great deal of resistance.

In 1944, when German losses were becoming harder to conceal, a Jewish Rescue Committee, the *Vaadah Ezra va Hazalah*, started secret negotiations with Adolf Eichmann. Using various contacts throughout Europe and Palestine, the organization hoped to obtain financial help to save the last remaining Jews in Hungary.

Dr. Rezső Kastner, a member of the *Vaadah Ezra va Hazalah* who has based in Budapest, undertook the negotiations. Although Eichmann refused to free all the Hungarian Jews, Kastner was able to persuade him to permit six hundred to depart for Palestine—at a ransom of $1,600,000. After the money was raised, Eichmann reluctantly agreed to release an additional thousand of his captives.

In the cities of Hungary, as in all the European ghettos, the Nazis had established Jewish councils. Their members were responsible to the Germans for the entire Jewish population and were forced, under the threat of death, to comply with S.S. orders. Many committed suicide rather than give in to the Germans' demands.

(Caption continues on page 72.)

Menu in Bergen-Belsen, 1944. Irsai. The contents of the cauldron, listed in Hungarian are: kolraby 8%, carrots 5%, meat (magnified) 1%, mussels 5%, potatoes (magnified) 3%, pumpkin 8%, turnips 20%, and water 50%.

KALARÁBÉ 8%
MUROK 5%
HÚS 1%
KAGYLÓ 5%
KRUMPLI 3%
TÖK 8%
MARHARÉPA 20%
VÍZ 50%

MENU DE BERGEN BELSEN 1944.

limitations, the ghetto dwellers lived with courage and hope, attempting to transcend the evil around them while safeguarding their own integrity.

Determined to let the world see the landscape of their tragedy, painters and writers feverishly recorded the doomed reality of the ghettos. By the act of documenting their life through drawings, paintings, and the written word, the artists—who often traded bread for ink, coal, paint, or paper—maintained morale within their community of friends and family. At the same time, the victims strengthened their own links with the past, fulfilling their emotional and psychological need to combat the Nazi brutality. Their feelings are best expressed in the words of one of their songs.

> My name is Israelik.
> I am the child of the ghetto.
> I am Israelik,
> An abandoned boy.
> Even though I am naked,
> I whistle and sing a song.
> Do not think the abandoned street
> Gave birth to me.
> Once I had a father and a mother.
> They took them away.
> Do not think I am joking.
> I remained like the wind in the street.

The Warsaw Ghetto has been the most fully documented of the East European ghettos. Historians have gathered valuable information on the valiant and tragic uprising that took place there when a handful of young men and women desperately resisted the Nazis' final assault.

The selection of deportees for the labor camps had been a terrible burden on the Jewish leadership, and now they were faced with yet another—deciding who should make up the "special transport" that would be saved. At first, they tried to ransom only children, but Eichmann vetoed this plan, claiming that such a group could not be smuggled across the borders into Switzerland without arousing too much suspicion.

Desperately, the council began to prepare a list, even as they continued to plead for more lives. At last, the names were collected—orthodox Jews, orphans, prominent Jewish figures, and families from Dr. Kastner's native city of Cluj. And so the bargain was completed. The "Kastner transport" proceeded to Bergen-Belsen disguised as a labor force. In accordance with Eichmann's secret plan, the group was then shipped to Switzerland.

Some time ago, I met one of the "chosen" survivors. Although he was a child at the time, this experience is still etched upon his soul. In Bergen-Belsen, his father exchanged cigarettes for two drawings by a camp artist named Irsai. These were carried with them to freedom; the fate of the artist is unknown.

Bergen-Belsen, July 9, 1944. Irsai. The reel of film shows parliament with the Star of David, symbolizing the Jewish Council; cattle cars with people crammed inside; barbed wire; barracks, a guard tower, and barbed wire; "tor," the Hungarian word for "lots," referring to those chosen for the special transport to Switzerland; a bowl and spoon (both empty); more "tor" lists; the last car of a train, with the caption 316, the number of people who were freed.

Despite the German practices of deliberate starvation, forced labor, and overwork; despite epidemics whose victims lay unburied, the Jews struggled to survive. They organized clandestine schools and cultural activities, soup kitchens and orphanages. Camouflaged workshops were actually centers which directed the smuggling of food from the Aryan side of the ghetto walls. Although mortality among the children was high, they were encouraged to continue attending classes.

The population within the ghetto was decimated. Starvation alone accounted for 43,000 deaths in 1941. But the dying was not fast enough for the Nazis, and a complete extermination program was prepared. The containment of Jews in the ghetto was only a prelude to "the final solution." The deportations, the "special treatment," the "resettlements," and the gas chambers were all shrouded in secrecy.

Resistance to the Nazi policies was not as great as it might have been because most of the people in the ghetto could not believe the truth of the concentration camps, even when confronted with evidence from those few who had seen for themselves and escaped. The truth became apparent only when it was too late.

Every day, Jews from the ghetto were loaded into freight cars and transported to Treblinka, Sobibor, Auschwitz, and Bergen-Belsen. Although they were allowed to take few personal possessions, many still believed that they were being resettled into eastern work camps.

Others, faced with immediate torture at the hands of the Gestapo, chose to die by their own hands. Their courage is vividly conveyed in this letter composed by ninety-three Jewish girls who poisoned themselves rather than submit to German soldiers:

Drawn in Buchenwald.

74

We have cleansed our bodies and purified our souls,
And now we are at peace.
    Death holds no terror; we go to meet it.
    We have served our God while alive;
    We know how to hallow him in death.
A deep covenant binds all ninety-three of us:
Together we studied God's Torah; together we
       shall die.
    We have chanted Psalms, and are comforted.
    We have confessed our sins, and are
         strengthened.
    We are now prepared to take our leave.
Let the unclean come to afflict us; we fear them not.
    We shall drink the poison and die, innocent and
        pure,
    As befits the daughters of Jacob.
To our mother Sarah we pray: ''Here we are!
    We have met the test of Isaac's Binding!
Pray with us for the people Israel.''
    Compassionate Father!
    Have mercy for Your people, who love You.
    For there is no more mercy in man.
Reveal your loving kindness.
Save your afflicted people.
    Cleanse and preserve Your world.
    The hour of Neilah approaches. Our hearts grow
       quiet.
We make but one request of our brethren, wherever
      they may be.
Say Kaddish for us, for all ninety-three, say
      Kaddish.

Drawn in Buchenwald.

The uprising in the Warsaw Ghetto did not take place until more than 300,000 Jews had been deported. About 70,000 remained behind, but they too were scheduled for extermination. Life in the ghetto was no longer measured even in terms of days and hours—there was no hope of survival. Babies were stuffed into suitcases and smuggled out. The nonfighting population hid in sewers and bunkers. Most of them would perish in the days to come.

Young Zionist units mobilized first, when a shipment of revolvers was smuggled over the walls of Parysowski Place. Under the heroic command of Mordecai Anilewicz, the Jews blocked the German attempt to clear the ghetto. There was no chance of victory for these desperate fighters; their only desire was to die with dignity. In May of 1943, the entire area was in flames; the Warsaw Ghetto had ceased to exist.

Just as Picasso's "Guernica" and the work of Goya, Bacon, and Daumier stir men's consciousness, so does the art that has survived the death and destruction of the ghettos. The painters of Lodz, Vilna, Warsaw, and other cities recorded their grey existence on canvas and gave their abysmal reality the permanence of written and painted images. In order to achieve this goal, the artists risked their lives.

Many of the artworks were concealed underground or smuggled out to non-Jewish friends for safekeeping. Drawn on scraps of paper, cardboard supply boxes, or any other surfaces that could be found, these works of poetry and art were tragic records of the ordeal that was the ghetto's history.

Drawn in Buchenwald.

The Partisan Song

Jewish resistance—whether in the ghettos, in Treblinka,
Auschwitz, Bergen-Belsen, or Sobibor—was often carried
out without help from other forces fighting the Nazis.
This was particularly true in eastern Europe, where deeply
rooted anti-Semitism reached even into the partisan
movement.

Overcoming almost insurmountable difficulties, a few
Jews still managed to escape to the forest and, after
"proving" themselves in battle, were allowed to join the
partisan brigades. As a young girl, I listened with admira-
tion and excitement to the stories told by a man who was
a great hero to me, the man my mother married after my
father's death. In my mind, I envisioned his tales of raids
against German communication lines, supply depots, and
troops. They were always set against the background of a
deep forest whose immensely dark and massive trees
sheltered the fighters.

No matter how small the unit or how limited its arms,
the Jewish partisans did not give up. Their song, which
eventually became the song of Jewish resistance through-
out Europe, was composed in Vilna by Hirsh Glik, a
young man who had been writing poetry since the age of
fifteen. Escaping from a German labor camp to the Vilna

Drawn in Buchenwald.

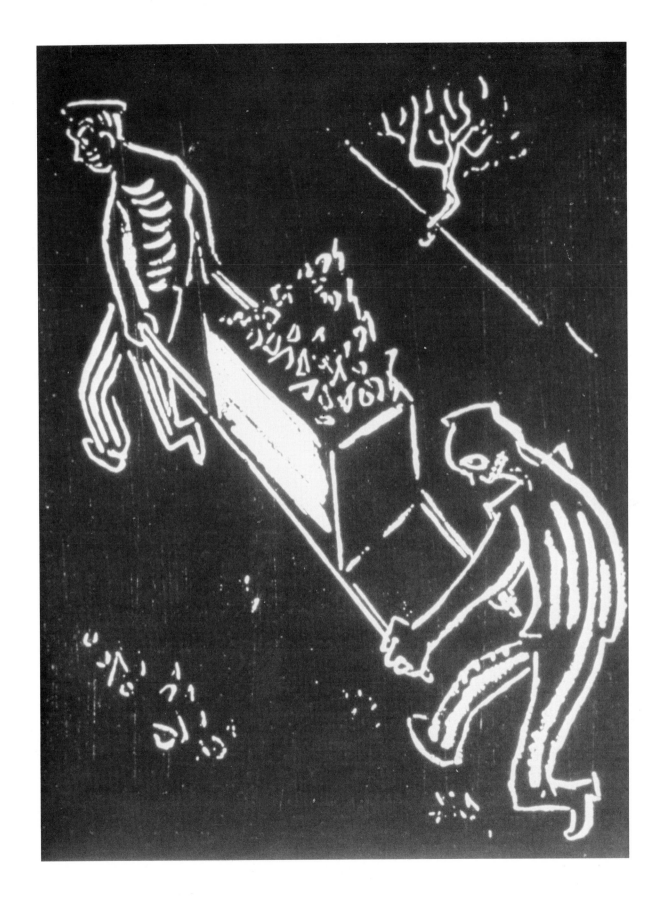

ghetto and from there into the woods, Glik continued to write until he was caught and sent to a concentration camp. Escaping once again, he was able to reach the forest and the safety of the partisans. There he died in action against the Germans.

His marching song, with music composed by the Russian Pokras brothers, was translated into many languages and sung by Jews all over the world.

Say not, it is the final road we tread,
Leaden skies will pass, and sun will shine instead.
Believe that freedom's hour will appear,
Our steps will tell the world that we are here.

From lands of palm and lands bedecked with snow
We came with all our people's pain and woe,
Where falls our martyr's blood into the earth,
Our courage and our hope shall have rebirth.

Tomorrow's dawn will robe our world in light,
Our yesterday will vanish with the night.
But if our freedom should arrive too late,
The world should know the meaning of our fate.

My muse is not a poet's playful dream,
I write in blood and not in ink my theme,
We sang it as our world went up in flame,
We sang it fighting to defend our name.

Say not, it is the final road we tread,
Leaden skies will pass, and sun will shine instead.
Believe that freedom's hour will appear,
Our steps will tell the world that we are here.

Drawn in Buchenwald.

ABOVE AND AT RIGHT: Drawn in Buchenwald.

84

Nelly Toll's Story

I shall never forget that sunny day in July 1941 when, as a small child, I watched the triumphal march of the German Army into Lwów. From the open window of my aunt's fourth floor apartment, my family watched the crowded streets. Below us, Polish men, women, and children threw flowers at the approaching German soldiers. In an atmosphere of joy and excitement, their laughter mixed with the sound of marching boots. Neither I, my five-year-old brother Janek, nor my four-year-old cousin Ninka knew exactly what to think. Certainly none of my family, and none of the Jewish population, suspected the tragedy that was to come.

Everything had happened so quickly. First there had been the Russian occupation and the confiscation of my parents' apartment, our furniture and paintings, and all our other belongings. My father had gone into hiding to avoid being deported to Siberia. Then there was the heavy bombing and our move, without my father, to my aunt's apartment. Finally, the Soviets retreated and the

From behind a curtained window, I could see the Germans all the time. Gestapo headquarters was across the street from our building. As the war progressed, it became a target for heavy bombing.

During the air raids, when the Germans and Poles fled to the cellar, my mother and I would run through the kitchen to the apartment's bathroom. We believed that it was safer because it was in the back of the building. There, at least, we couldn't see anything.

During one of the heaviest air raids, after Mr. and Mrs. Z had gone to the cellar, a piece of shrapnel landed on my mother's ankle as we rushed through the kitchen. Limping toward the sink, she removed the metal, wrapped a thin towel around her foot, and continued on to the bathroom. As I sat on the edge of the large tub, it vibrated with the sounds of the bombs that were dropping all around the building.

Our Hiding Place. Nelly Toll.

Germans took their place. A vague, unknown fear descended on our family. When my father came to visit, I overheard my parents whispering together.

Within the first few days of the German occupation, Jews were snatched on the streets by Polish and German police. Often they were beaten and forced to clean the rubble, much to the enjoyment of the Polish population. Anti-Semitism had been a part of Polish life long before it was fanned by the Nazis. My grandmother told frightening stories about pogroms that had taken place long before I was born.

The Nazis rounded up men, women, and children and carried them off. The streets became unsafe, and people hid in their apartments. Except for my teenaged cousin Sewer, who did not "look Jewish," we children were forbidden to leave the building. A dark cloud descended on our lives.

With the rest of the Jewish population, my family was given several hours' notice to move out of our apartment and into a newly formed ghetto, which was heavily guarded by the police. No one was allowed to leave the

"I remember when my mother made all my clothes. She knitted dresses and sweaters for me."

One day, as we sat in the kitchen with Mrs. Z, the doorbell rang. We ran to our room, Mrs. Z quickly turned the key, and the room was locked. Only then did she open the front door. But my mother had dropped a ball of wool on the kitchen floor and had forgotten to let go of the end. Although we heard a neighbor's voice in the kitchen, my mother, without thinking, continued to pull on the red wool. The ball began to roll over the kitchen floor toward our door. At that instant, I ripped the strand in two. In the kitchen, on the other side of the door, Mrs. Z picked up the ball, and the wool disappeared underneath the door. Our lives were suspended in that small crack of space that separated the wooden floor from the bottom of the door. Luck was with us. The suspicious incident was never reported to the Gestapo.

The Knitting Girl. Nelly Toll.

area without a special permit. Actions and deportations followed. I remember hearing that many labor camps were really places where Jews were put to death in gas chambers, but I don't think I fully understood the meaning of these words.

For a while, my parents placed me in a secret hiding place with a Christian family. On my return to the ghetto, I learned that my brother Janek, my aunt, and my baby cousin Ninka had been seized. Seeing that I was terribly shaken, my father tried to comfort me. He said that some people escaped the gas chambers by jumping from the transport trains.

Fear struck all of us in the ghetto. A few made attempts to hide their children with Christian families; some tried to escape into the woods and join the Russian partisans. Others were seized. Both my cousins, Sewer and Karol, were caught in a Nazi round-up and murdered. Aunt Hana took poison. My grandparents were lucky; they just died.

Realizing the hopelessness of the situation, my father made arrangements for my mother and I to escape. A

Shut in my room, recalling fresh outdoor days, I remembered that even without sunshine beautiful sunflowers had grown in the shade of the forest near Szelskie, the village from which we had hoped to be escorted to Hungary. I had seen the flowers when my mother and I had fled from a German round-up.

As I drew the sunflowers, I felt myself surrounded by earthworms, small creeping animals, wild vegetation, and marshy waters, all growing taller and taller in the shadows of the twisted trees. It could have been very peaceful in this damp, swampy area if it hadn't been for the crows. Circling around, following the sounds of shooting, they descended to look for dead flesh. I can still hear their crowing as the Angel of Death hovered near us. Another massacre had been completed.

Sunflowers Growing in the Shadow. Nelly Toll.

well-paid German major was to have helped twenty Jews cross the border into Hungary, but once we arrived in Szelskie, the small Polish village that was to have been our first stop, the major suddenly disappeared and the Nazis staged a round-up. For a week we hid in the peasants' barns and then escaped into the nearby woods. After the raid was over, my mother, and a handful of others who had survived the action, decided that it was wiser to return to the ghetto.

After many brushes with death, my father managed to arrange a hiding place for my mother and me. In 1943, we crossed the forbidden streets into a residential area of Lwów that was occupied by many Germans. On a prear- ranged signal, we entered a building where Christian friends of my father's would hide us until the end of the war. My father was to join us after he had seen to the rest of the family.

Mr. Z built us a hiding place inside a blind window that had been bricked over many years earlier to keep the cold air from coming in. Fortunately, the window was

My mother and I spent hours playing dominoes. In those dark hours, behind the locked doors, on the other side of the world, my mother tried to ease my fear and loneliness. She became my girlfriend and my teacher.

Playing Dominoes. Nelly Toll.

now only visible from the inside of the room. Mr. Z covered the ''blind'' window with boards, painted them beige to match the other walls, and cut out an opening barely large enough for my mother and me to climb in. When strangers called, we would hide there, trembling with fear, hoping that no one would lift the Persian rug that hung on the wall ''as a decoration'' to cover the entrance to our shelter.

Our hiding place was in a locked room off the apartment's kitchen. It was only safe for a routine examination. When German or Polish officials were making an inspection, Mrs. Z would signal us by speaking loud and clear as she looked slowly in her kitchen drawers for the key. Numb with fright, my mother and I would tiptoe swiftly across the room to our window. Holding each other tight, we would wait with terror for the moments to pass.

Most of the occupants of the apartment building were Germans, and many of those were members of the Gestapo. One of the few Poles was Miss W, a widow friend of Mrs. Z. Risking her life, she supplied me with

Standing behind the curtained window, I watched the children playing and wished that I too could go outside. Instead, I visited the children on paper; I took a walk with them on paper.

Small green leaves covered the trees and sunshine splashed the streets. Spring was greeting Lwów, casting warm shadows on crowded P Square. Little girls' boots were replaced by shoes, scarves were discarded, jackets were opened. The children's laughter matched the weather. A balloon floated past our window and almost touched the bricks.

(Caption continues on page 96.)

A Happy Summer Day. Nelly Toll.

books, paper, and watercolors that she bought in stores in distant parts of the city. Our area, which was a fashionable district popular with German officers, was too dangerous a place to make such purchases, lest they arouse suspicion.

For thirteen frightening months we never left the apartment. Aware of the constant danger of discovery, knowing that the Gestapo paid substantial rewards for every person reported, my mother and I lived in paralyzing fear. During those dark hours, my mother encouraged me to continue the reading, writing, and painting that I had always enjoyed.

Focussing on my past and visualizing a better future, my pictures did not reflect the Nazi brutality and the suffering that I had seen around me. Only symbolically did they reflect our precarious existence and our despair. By shutting out the reality that I could not understand, I was able to live in a make-believe landscape.

Since those days, I have seen other drawings done by children in ghettos and camps, particularly those from

I watched the world outside intently, always hoping to see my father suddenly emerge from the crowd, walking briskly toward our building, his hat pulled low over his eyes. My father had visited us twice before. He had stayed only a short time, promising to return when he was sure that the rest of the family had found a safe hiding place.

(Caption continues on page 98.)

A Happy Summer Day. Nelly Toll.

Terezin. Anyone who has studied them will notice that the girls' artwork is usually quite different from the boys'. The girls focussed more often on memories of the lost past, filling their pictures with images of gardens, butterflies, princesses, castles, cottages, families, and friends—everything that recalled love and happiness. In contrast, the boys depicted the horrible reality around them. Their pictures are alive with S.S. men and transports; they pulsate with the rhythms of death and burial.

Some children expressed their emotional needs through imagination and fantasy; others recorded the harsh realities of the world around them. Although my drawings often showed imaginary worlds, my diary was a true record of the events of those times. If I was discovered, I wanted the world to read it and to know what had happened. But in my artwork I composed a reality devoid of cruelty. Comforted by these scenes, I was able to preserve an image of humanity, kindness, and, most of all, hope, as a means of survival.

In my diary, I wrote: ''From my bed I can see the stars. In the distance and beyond them is God. I trust him. I know that He can see me even in the dark and that if I pray He might grant my wish.''

But I never saw my father again.

In June 1944, we were liberated by the Red Army.

A Happy Summer Day. Nelly Toll.

Retrospective

Although the focus of this book is the artwork produced in the camps and ghettos during the Holocaust, one cannot ignore the impact of the Nazi atrocities on the artists of the post-war period. To fully explore this influence would, of course, encompass several books, but it seems appropriate to close this view of the Holocaust artists with a glimpse of the work produced by two of their spiritual descendants.

Mauricio Lasansky has no direct experience of the Holocaust, but he is inextricably linked to it through his tradition as an artist and his ever-growing realization of the enormity of the Nazis' crimes. His drawings are an eloquent expression of the anguish and rage that various artists throughout the world have felt in reaction to what took place in wartime Europe.

It is only fitting, however, that I have chosen to close Without Surrender *with the work of a survivor. Jan De Ruth, who endured five concentration camps, is one of the few people who remain as a living link to the experiences of the past. As an artist and as a human being, he has a special message to convey, an affirmation of the essential dignity and strength of will which lie within the human spirit—and an equally strong resolve that, as his painting's title reminds us, the horrors that took place in the Holocaust should be* No More.

In 1967, while serving as a guide at the Philadelphia Museum of Art, I was able to conduct many visitors through a powerful exhibition of drawings by Mauricio Lasansky, one of the most influential figures in American graphic arts and until recently Professor of Art and chairman of the printmaking department at the University of Iowa.

Mauricio Lasansky was born in Argentina in 1914 and came to America in 1943, at the age of 28. From 1961 to 1966, he worked on *The Nazi Drawings*, which he has described as "an instinctive reaction" to the Holocaust. This series of drawings, some of which are as large as six by four feet, was executed with lead pencil, red and brown pigments, and turpentine wash on brown and white commercial paper. Using these ordinary materials, Lasansky has created a searing indictment of twentieth-century man, reminding us that the atrocities known as the Holocaust took place a mere thirty-five years ago.

Nazi Drawing #26. Mauricio Lasansky. Pencil, brown and red pigment, turpentine. 45½ × 43 in.

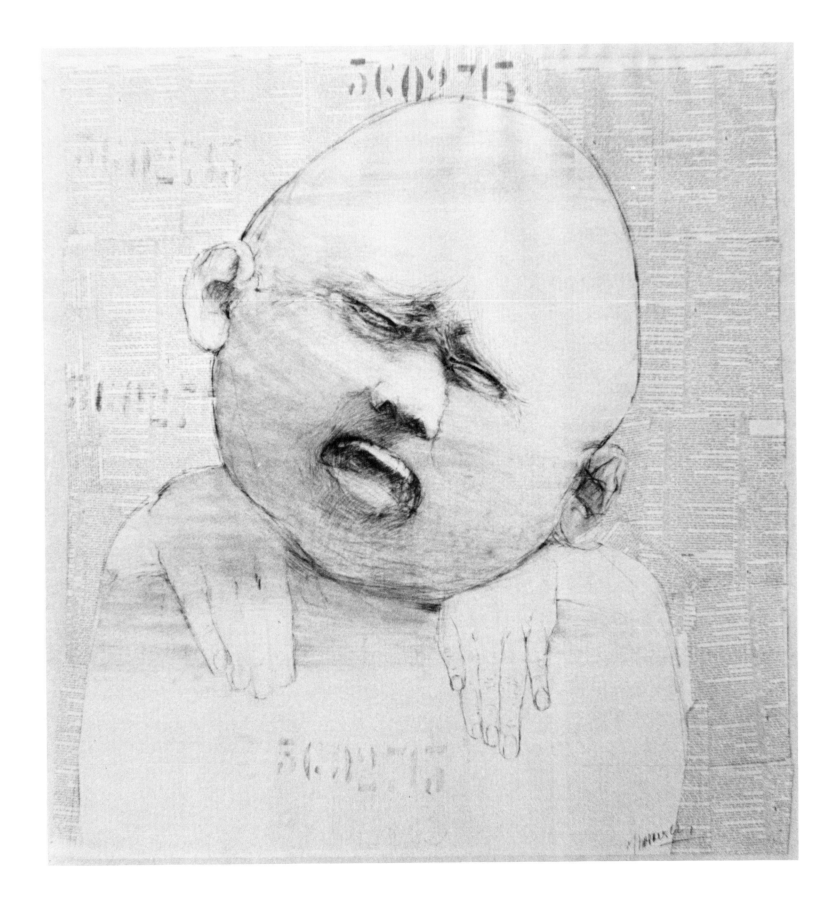

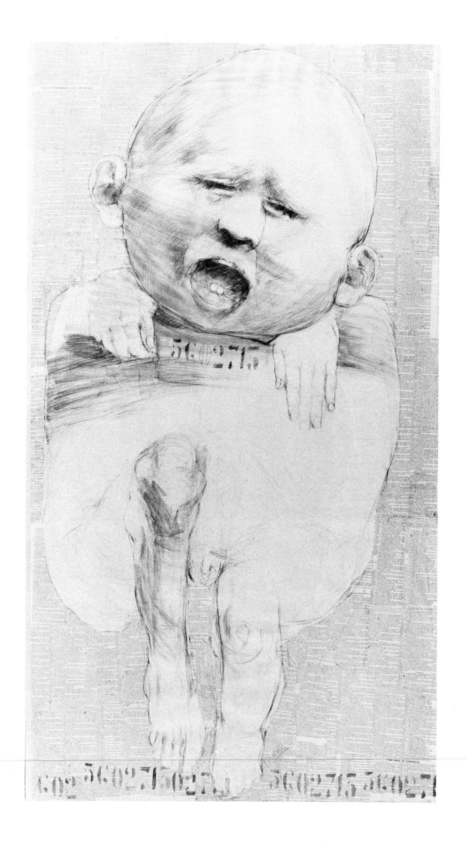

Nazi Drawing #28. Mauricio Lasansky. Pencil, brown and red pigment, turpentine. 82 × 45 in.

Nazi Drawing #29. Mauricio Lasansky. Pencil, brown and red pigment, turpentine. 78 × 45 in.

Nazi Drawing #17. Mauricio Lasansky. Pencil, red and brown pigment, turpentine. 75 × 45 in.

Nazi Drawing #6. Mauricio Lasansky. Pencil, red and brown pigment, turpentine. 71 × 23 in.

Nazi Drawing #8. Mauricio Lasansky. Pencil, brown and red pigment, turpentine. 69 × 25 ½ in.

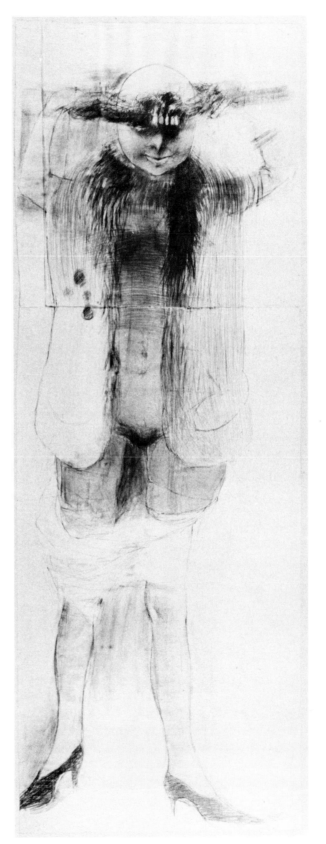

JAN DE RUTH:

"I arrived in Auschwitz from Teresienstadt in September of 1944. Within hours of our arrival, the reality of the place began to dawn on us. Although we were within the sight and smell of the crematoria, we could not and did not want to believe what was happening. We had to face the fact that most of those we ever loved or even knew were dead. Mothers, fathers, children, brothers, sisters, grandparents, lovers—all had died.

"Some of us 'needed' to survive, survival being a question of instinct and perhaps honor—to endure and to live once more the way we had before the Germans took it upon themselves to decide who was to live and who was to die. Some could not endure the pain. Some just gave up and died slowly, or ended up in the gas chamber. Others could be part of life another day.

"This man was a stranger, just another man among us. His wife and child had died in a gas chamber. When the realization of that fact penetrated to the depths of his soul, he turned from us and walked into the electrified wires that surrounded the camp. That sort of act was not uncommon.

"As he hung there, electrocuted, the guards from the watch towers fired a few rounds to make sure—to make sure of what? These wires were not the borders of Auschwitz, they merely separated one compound from another. They let him hang on the wires, perhaps for a day, perhaps a week. It's difficult to recall how long; my memories of days and weeks in Auschwitz have become just one dark night.

"I am writing of this, the only painting I did of four and a half years of moving from camp to camp, during a beautiful Berkshire sunset. It is not unlike the chimney's glow that still lives within us."

Jan De Ruth was born in Karlsbad, Czechoslovakia in 1922. During the war, he was interned in five different concentration camps. "The only things we had," De Ruth recalls, "were the few pieces of cloth we wore." Once, when he was transferred to Germany with a labor detail, he managed to steal a pencil from the camp supervisor. With it, he drew a mother and child on a scrap of paper he had found in the factory where he worked. He filled in the drawing with shadings of coffee, using his finger as a brush. De Ruth exchanged the sketch for a piece of bread from a camp guard— his first "sale" as an artist.

After four escape attempts, Jan De Ruth was returned to his native Czechoslovakia in March of 1945. There he finally succeeded in escaping from the Nazis. Following the war, he managed to flee to England and later emigrated to the United States.

No More. Jan De Ruth. 1948. 64 × 48 in.